Grades 4 up.

Penn Hills Library
240 Aster Street
Pittsburgh, PA 15235

science@work
Crime

FORGERIES, Fingerprints, and FORENSICS

By Janice Parker

RSVP

RAINTREE STECK-VAUGHN
P U B L I S H E R S
A Steck-Vaughn Company

Austin, Texas

www.steck-vaughn.com

Published by Raintree Steck-Vaughn, an imprint of Steck-Vaughn Company

Library of Congress Cataloging-in-Publication Data

Parker, Janice.
    Forgeries, fingerprints, and forensics: the science of crime /
  by Janice Parker.
        p.   cm. — (Science [at] work)
  In ser. statement "[at]" appears as the at symbol.
  Includes bibliographical references (p. 46) and index.
  Summary: A basic introduction to the many ways in which police and detectives use science to fight crime, discussing video surveillance, burglar alarms, ballistics, autopsies, handwriting analysis, and other methods.
  ISBN 0-7398-0133-3
  1. Forensic sciences—Juvenile literature. 2. Criminal investigation—Juvenile literature. 3. Crime prevention—Juvenile literature. [1. Forensic sciences. 2. Criminal investigation.] I. Title. II. Series: Science [at] work (Austin, Tex.)
HV873.8.P37   1999
363.25—DC21   98-55476
                                        CIP
                                        AC

Printed and bound in Canada
1 2 3 4 5 6 7 8 9 0   03 02 01 00 99

Project Coordinator
Ann Sullivan
Content Validator
Lois Edwards
Design
Warren Clark
Copy Editors
Rennay Craats
Krista McLuskey
Leslie Strudwick
Layout and Illustration
Chantelle Sales

Photograph Credits
Every reasonable effort has been made to trace ownership and to obtain permission to reprint copyright material. The publishers would be pleased to have any errors or omissions brought to their attention so that they may be corrected in subsequent printings.

Peter Battistoni/*Vancouver Sun*: page 39; **Dave Butler**: page 12 left; **Calgary Police Service**: pages 4 top, 10, 11, 26 top, 43 left; **Gary Neil Corbett**: page 21; **Corel Corporation**: cover top, pages 9 bottom, 18 bottom, 19, 37 top, 40, 41; **CP Picture Archive (Moe Doiron)**: page 34; **Nick Didlick/*Vancouver Sun***: page 35; **Robert Exeter**: page 38; **Eyewire Incorporated**: pages 6 left, 7; **Federal Bureau of Investigation**: pages 4 middle, 27 bottom, 42 left; **Forensic Audio Analysis**: page 33; **John Fowler**: page 18 top; **Orange County Sheriff-Coroner, Forensic Science Center**: page 16; **Resource Protection Services Incorporated**: pages 4 bottom, 9 top; **Royal Canadian Mounted Police**: cover bottom, pages 14, 15, 20, 22, 23 right, 30, 31, 37 bottom, 43 right; **Shield Security Services**: page 6 top; **Tom Stack and Associates**: cover background, pages 12 top, 13, 23 top, 24, 25, 26 left, 28, 29, 32 (Tom and Therisa Stack); **David Sweet**: page 36; **Mark van Manen/*Vancouver Sun***: page 17.

Contents

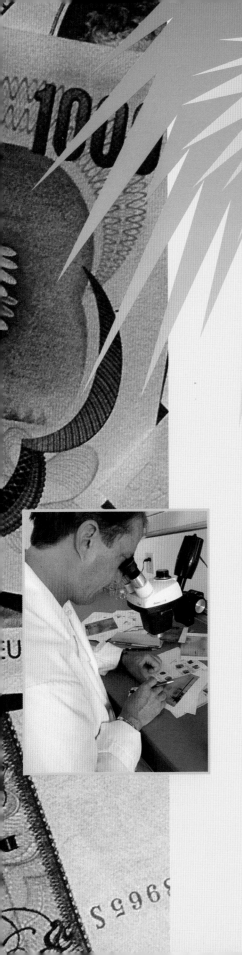

Have you ever wondered why people commit crimes,

how the police catch criminals,

or what we do to prevent crime from happening?

Every society in the world has crime. Wherever there are people, there are crimes committed. Science plays an important role in crime. With the help of science, we can prevent many crimes from happening. If a crime occurs, science helps us to investigate it. Science also helps us to understand how the crime took place, catch criminal suspects, and make sure that a court jury is convinced of the suspect's guilt.

FINDING LINKS

Society

Crime affects society in many different ways. Criminals steal, destroy property, and even harm or kill people. Fighting crime is one of the top priorities for most governments.

The Environment

Would you like to help prevent or solve crimes? There are many careers relating to crime, such as police officer, detective, lawyer, and security guard. Many people whose work is to investigate crimes are scientists. Forensic biologists, **DNA** specialists, and medical examiners all work with the police to solve crimes.

Technology

Technology gives us many tools to help prevent crimes from happening. Technology also helps police investigate crimes to find out who committed them. Since criminals also use technology, police and other law enforcement officials must keep up-to-date with knowledge about new technological inventions that might be used to commit crimes.

Careers

Many things in the environment help investigators as they try to solve crimes. Living things, such as insects and plants, often give clues as to where or when a crime occurred. Dirt and snow will often contain footprints or tire tracks that may be valuable clues in an investigation.

Preventing Crime

"Smile! You're on camera!"

Many people believe that the job of the police should be to catch criminals and provide evidence that will later ensure the criminals go to jail. Science helps the police do this. But science also helps prevent crimes from happening in the first place. It costs money to solve crimes. We hope to reduce the number of crimes committed, and save money, by having good methods to discourage criminals from acting. There are many inventions that allow us to prevent crimes. Alarms, locks, and X-ray machines are examples of things that are used to prevent people from committing crimes.

Are you being watched?

Many businesses and office buildings have security cameras. Security cameras take photographs or videos of everything that is happening in the building. The cameras are often hidden or placed so that most people do not notice them. In some buildings, security guards watch monitors to see what is viewed by the video cameras. Security guards make sure that no crime is occurring. A guard who sees a person steal on the monitor can go into the store to catch the shoplifter.

In other places, no one watches what happens, but police can later check the videos to see if they can identify a criminal. People are sometimes robbed at automated bank machines. By watching the videos that are taken by the machines, police often can identify and catch the thieves.

Security cameras hidden in automated bank machines keep a record of the people who use the machine. In the event of a crime, the police can review images from these cameras.

BYTE-SIZED FACT

Surveillance cameras that are as small as the head of a pin are now available. These cameras can be hidden in clocks, picture frames, or smoke detectors. Some cameras can clearly film objects that are 3 feet (1 m) away in total darkness. Others can pick up sound as well as pictures. Cameras can be hooked up to televisions or computer screens to view photographs.

How Do Burglar Alarms Work?

Burglar alarms can help prevent thieves from breaking into homes, offices, and other buildings.

A burglar alarm system uses sensors to detect anyone who enters a building. If these sensors detect that someone has entered or is in the building, an alarm is set off.

Burglar alarms often work by emitting loud noises, which are intended to scare away intruders. Burglars do not want anything to bring attention to their activities. Some alarm systems are connected to the police or to a security company. These alarms may or may not make a noise. When they go off, the police or security officers are sent to the

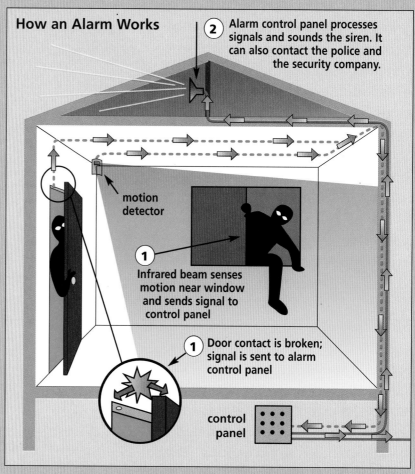

How an Alarm Works

2 Alarm control panel processes signals and sounds the siren. It can also contact the police and the security company.

motion detector

1 Infrared beam senses motion near window and sends signal to control panel

1 Door contact is broken; signal is sent to alarm control panel

control panel

building to see what has happened. There are two main types of burglar alarms: magnetic and infrared.

Magnetic burglar alarms use sensors placed on each window and door of a building. The sensors are made of two parts held together by sealed magnets. If one of the doors or windows is opened, the two parts of the sensor are pulled apart. A signal is then sent to the alarm system, and the alarm is set off.

Infrared burglar alarms can sense movement within a building. They do this by sensing heat, or infrared radiation, which is given off by all people and animals. We cannot see heat energy, but infrared sensors can detect it. The sensors even work in the dark. If the sensors detect any movement in areas where there should be no people, an alarm is set off.

BYTE-SIZED FACT
Some infrared sensors can tell the difference between humans and animals. This means that an alarm will be set off only by people, not by security dogs or pets.

Are airplanes safe from criminals?

Many people travel in airplanes. Airport security helps to protect air passengers from hijackers or bombs on the plane. At nearly every airport in the world, people boarding a plane must go through a security check. All the luggage is put through an **X-ray scanner**. X-ray scanners allow security personnel to see through a closed suitcase or box and look at everything that is inside. Security personnel then check any luggage that looks like it might contain weapons, bombs, or other illegal items, such as drugs.

X-ray scanners work very well for luggage, but they are not used on humans. Too many X-rays can harm humans. Instead, people walk through a doorway containing a **metal detector**.

Metal detectors have sensors that set off an alarm if there is any metal on a person. They are designed to find guns or knives hidden in clothing.

Every person who boards an airplane must first walk through an X-ray scanner.

BYTE-SIZED FACT Most metal detectors are made to go off only if large metal objects like knives are sensed. However, a detector may be set off by coins left in a pocket or even by metal dental fillings.

How do police catch people driving over the speed limit?

Every year, thousands of people are killed in automobile accidents. Many of these accidents could have been avoided if drivers had not driven faster than the posted speed limit. The faster a vehicle moves, the more damage it will cause if it hits another object. In an effort to prevent accidents, police give tickets to people who drive over the speed limit.

To catch speeders, police often stand or park in a place that is not readily visible to drivers. The police officer holds a speed gun, which is pointed in the direction of oncoming vehicles. A speed gun does not fire bullets, but uses radar to determine how fast a car is moving. A radar gun works by sending out radio waves. By sensing how fast the waves bounce back, a radar gun can tell the speed of a vehicle.

Police officers use speed guns to determine how fast cars are moving.

There is another machine that catches speeders without the help of a police officer. A radar camera works the same way as a speed gun. It determines how fast a vehicle is moving. If the radar senses that the vehicle is going too fast, the camera takes a picture of the car and its license plate. A speeding ticket is then mailed to the owner of the vehicle.

BYTE-SIZED FACT

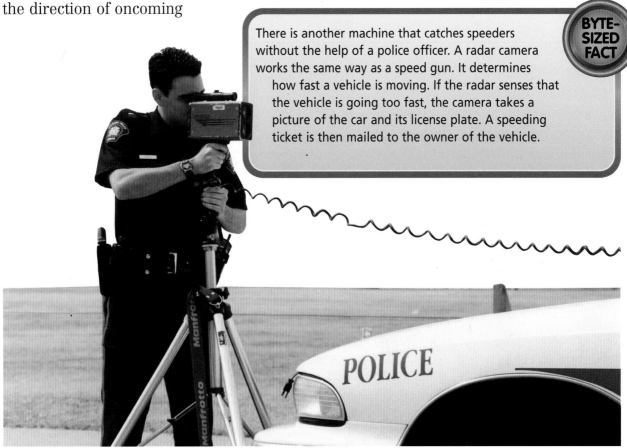

Law Enforcement Officers

If you like the idea of preventing crime and protecting people, you might want to become a law enforcement officer. Police officer or detective are just two of the many different jobs in law enforcement.

The police officer's most important tasks are to protect people and catch suspected criminals. Some police officers patrol certain areas on foot or in their vehicles to make sure that no crimes are being committed. They respond when someone calls the emergency line for help. Police officers also help to educate the public about crimes and ways to make communities and homes safer.

Detectives catch people who commit crimes and identify victims. They are sometimes called criminal investigators because they investigate, or find information about, crimes. They look for **evidence** and interview witnesses and suspects. Once detectives have found enough evidence, police can arrest a suspect.

One of the jobs of a law enforcement officer is to ensure that drivers obey the rules of the road.

Investigating Crime

"May I see your license, please?"

Not all crimes can be prevented, so law enforcement officials often need to do a criminal investigation to learn who committed a crime and how. The first step in investigating a crime is usually responding to a telephone call. Police immediately go to the crime scene. They seal off the area and do not allow anyone to enter. The scene of the crime is photographed. Fingerprints and other types of evidence are quickly and carefully collected and taken to the police laboratory. Police use this evidence to answer questions about the crime.

What is a crime scene?

A crime scene is the location where a crime took place. Examples of crime scenes are a building that has been broken into, or the place where an injured or dead person has been found.

If a crime scene in a murder case is a home, the crime scene includes the room where the body was found, as well as the rest of the house. Police search the entire crime scene for clues that may help them to solve the crime.

Crime scenes are blocked off so that the evidence will not be disturbed. Even the most careful criminals usually leave clues behind. Before the evidence is collected, police take photographs of the area. They then collect anything that could be a clue to the crime. Police wear plastic gloves whenever they collect a piece of evidence so that they do not leave their own fingerprints on the object. They place all evidence in separate plastic bags that are then labeled. Investigators change their gloves often so that they do not move tiny bits from one piece of evidence to another piece of evidence. After all the evidence has been collected, it is taken to a police laboratory for analysis.

Crime scenes are sealed to make sure that evidence is not moved or lost. The exact location of evidence is important in determining how a crime was committed.

Forensic Scientist

Are you interested in helping to solve crimes through the use of science?

If so, you may want to consider becoming a forensic scientist. **Forensic science** helps investigators find and analyze evidence that can be used in a court of law.

Forensic scientists use technology to examine physical evidence found during criminal investigations. They usually work in police laboratories and play an important part in solving crimes. There are many different types of forensic scientists, each with a specialty. Here are a few examples:

Forensic Pathologist

Forensic pathologists are doctors who examine bodies to find out how and when death occurred. They look for wounds, bruises, and other physical signs that might show the cause of death. In cases in which police do not know how a person died, a forensic pathologist examines the body.

Forensic Anthropologist

Forensic anthropologists specialize in studying bones found at crime scenes. They help to identify the victim and the way in which he or she died.

Forensic Biologist

Forensic biologists study body fluids, such as blood or saliva, that have been left at a crime scene. Some biologists are experts in studying DNA. They are called DNA specialists.

Forensic Entomologist

Entomologists study insects. Forensic entomologists study insects at a crime scene. They try to determine the time and location of the death of a murder victim by examining the insects that are found on the victim's body.

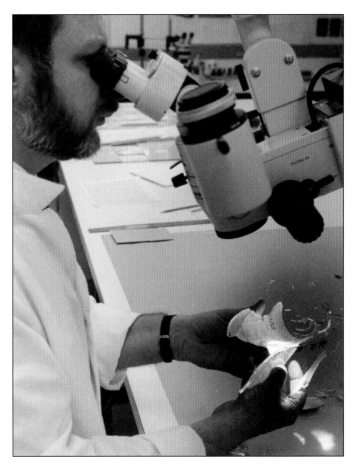

A forensic scientist analyzes pieces of glass to see whether they match evidence that was collected at a crime scene.

How do police know which gun was used in a crime?

If police find a weapon near a crime scene, they need to find out whether it was used to commit the crime. To do this, police look at the bullets found in a victim or at a crime scene. The study of guns and bullets in criminal investigations is called **ballistics**.

Unused bullets are smooth on the outside. When a bullet is fired from a gun, it is scratched as it moves through the barrel of the gun. Lines and ridges are left on the bullet. Bullets fired from the same gun have the same ridges. If police find a gun they think may have been used in a crime, they will fire some bullets from that gun. If the ridges on the bullets they fire match those on the bullet found at the crime scene, police know that gun was used during the crime.

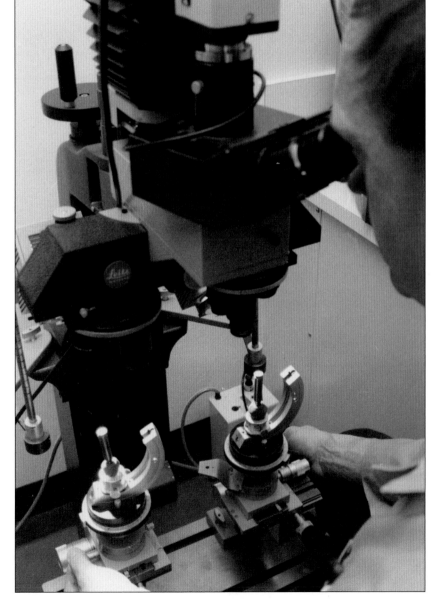

To determine whether two bullets were fired from the same gun, police examine the bullets, looking for scratches made by the barrel of the gun. If both bullets have the same scratches, police know they were fired from the same gun.

How do scientists determine how someone died?

An **autopsy** is often performed when someone dies, especially if the death is suspicious. Usually an autopsy can help tell how and when a person died. Autopsies are done by forensic pathologists in a medical laboratory.

To do an autopsy, a pathologist first looks closely at the body of the dead person. Bruises, wounds, or marks of any kind are photographed and described in writing. If there are gunshot wounds, the pathologist can help determine what type of gun was used and how close the gun was to the victim when it was fired. Any pieces of bullet found are removed.

If there are knife wounds, the pathologist counts the wounds and can sometimes determine whether the killer is right-handed or left-handed. Bruise marks around the neck usually mean that the victim was strangled. The bruises are sometimes measured to determine the size of the hands of the killer.

After examining the outside of the body, the pathologist cuts the body open. The organs are removed and weighed. Any food in the stomach is examined. At this point, scientists also check to see whether there are any poisons present by testing body fluids.

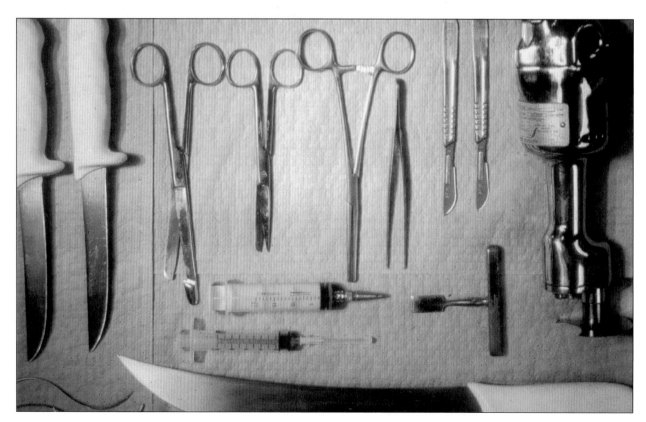

When a person dies under suspicious circumstances, an autopsy is performed to determine exactly what caused the person's death.

How do scientists determine the time of death?

When investigating a murder case, pathologists must try to figure out exactly when the victim died. This information helps narrow down suspects. To estimate the time of death, pathologists look for several things:

After death, body temperature steadily cools down until it is the same as the temperature of the surrounding area. By understanding how fast a body cools down under different conditions, scientists can roughly estimate the time of death.

Lividity refers to the color of areas on a dead body that darken after death. Gravity causes blood in a victim's body to settle in the areas that are closest to the ground. Lividity usually occurs half an hour to 3 hours after death. Scientists can tell that a body was moved after that time if the dark marks are not close to the ground.

About 3 to 5 hours after death, the muscles in a body usually become stiff. This condition is known as **rigor mortis**. Rigor mortis disappears about 24 to 36 hours after death. If rigor mortis is present in a victim, scientists know that the death happened in the previous day and a half.

Decomposition is the breakdown of cells in a plant or animal that is no longer alive. This begins immediately after death. Scientists are often able

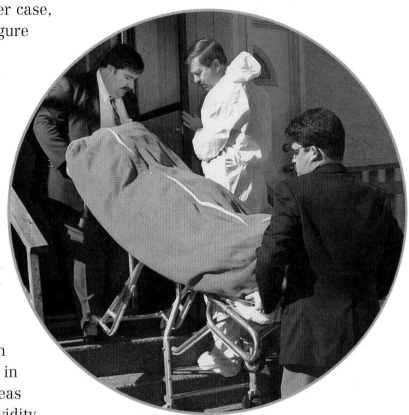

Pathologists have many ways to figure out the time of a person's death.

to estimate the time of death by looking at how much decomposition has taken place. Decomposition is caused by bacteria and fungi that cannot survive on a living organism. They cause the body to change color and produce odors. Insects also cause decomposition. They lay eggs on the body. When the eggs hatch, the larvae feed on the skin and tissues.

Can Insects Help Us Tell the Time of a Person's Death?

Many living things are useful to forensic scientists. Insects are especially helpful during murder investigations.

Insects can help us figure out approximately when and where a person died.

Soon after a person dies, some insects begin to lay eggs on the body. Once the eggs hatch, the young insects, or larvae, will eat the dead tissue. Different types of insects lay their eggs at different times. Some insects lay their eggs soon after a person has died. Others will not lay their eggs until a body has been dead for months.

All insects have life cycles. Many insects, for example, begin their lives as eggs, hatch into larvae, and then change into their adult form. By determining the insects' stage of life, scientists can estimate how long a person has been dead.

Insects such as maggots (above) or flies on a body tell forensic scientists how long the person has been dead.

How do investigators identify forgeries and counterfeits?

Forgeries are fakes. They are copies of objects that are made to trick people into believing that they are genuine. Criminals have made copies of famous paintings, jewelry, and important documents, such as wills. Criminals sometimes also forge a signature on a check or credit card receipt in order to steal money or merchandise.

Scientists use many different methods to find out if something is real or a forgery. Most artists have a way of painting or drawing that makes their work different and difficult to copy. Paints and other materials that are used today are different from those used many years ago. By analyzing the chemicals in a painting, scientists can often tell whether or not the painting is real.

People also make fake money, called counterfeit money. New technologies such as color **laser** printers make it easier for criminals to make copies of money. Most countries add details to their money that make it very difficult to copy.

Investigators look for these special features when they are trying to find out if money is real or counterfeit. For instance, some bills now have

Criminals often copy famous paintings and sell them for a great deal of money. This is called art forgery.

Some criminals make counterfeit money and try to pass it off as real. Many countries add special features to their money to make it harder to duplicate.

small **holograms**, which cannot be copied easily. Most bills also have words written on them in very small letters. These tiny words are very difficult to copy. Another way to identify counterfeit money is to test the paper and ink. Counterfeiters cannot easily get the same materials that are used to make real money.

What can scientists tell from a piece of writing?

Every person's handwriting is unique. Even though handwriting can change depending on a person's mood or how quickly a person writes, certain details about the writing stay the same. Police analyze handwriting to learn more about a crime. The study of handwriting is called **graphology**.

Handwriting experts, or graphologists, are trained to spot differences between people's handwriting. By comparing several different pieces of writing, they can often decide who wrote a ransom letter or forged a name on a check.

Sometimes graphologists help with criminal investigations. People who suffer from certain mental illnesses, and who may be more likely to commit crimes, sometimes have a specific type of handwriting. If someone is receiving threatening letters from an unknown person, a graphologist can look at the writing and help determine if the person writing the letters is dangerous. A graphologist may also be able to look at a letter and know whether the writer was lying or telling the truth.

Differences in handwriting help graphologists identify forged checks.

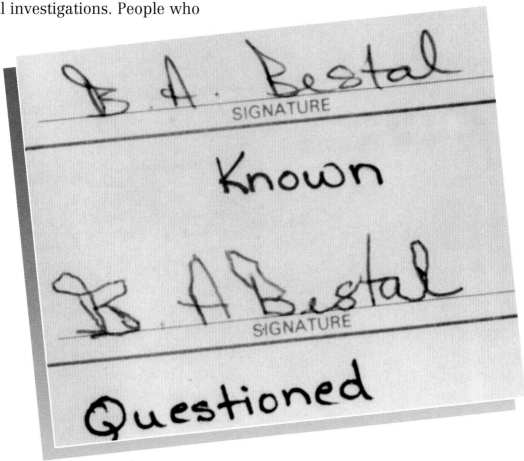

Who Solves International Crimes?

Some crimes affect people in more than one country or even people all around the world. It is difficult for police in one country to solve a crime that affects many countries.

Interpol, or the International Criminal Police Organization, is a group that fights major crime and protects people around the world. Interpol was founded in 1923, and its headquarters is located in Lyon, France.

Interpol focuses mainly on international crime, especially the drug trade, computer crime, art theft, and terrorism. Investigators at Interpol have detailed information on millions of international criminals. Interpol helps other police organizations around the world by sending them information on criminals and crimes. There are 176 police organizations around the world that belong to Interpol.

Interpol fights international crimes, such as terrorism and art theft.

BYTE-SIZED FACT Three of the most powerful national crime prevention organizations in the world are the FBI in the United States, New Scotland Yard in Great Britain, and the Sûreté Nationale in France. Most other countries also have national police forces.

How do cloth fibers help police investigate crimes?

As people move, small fibers fall from their clothing. These fibers float in the air and attach themselves to other objects or people. If you sit in a car, for example, you will likely pick up fibers from the material on the seats or the floor. These tiny fibers can help link a suspect to a crime.

Fibers are usually difficult to see without help from a magnifying glass or microscope. Police officers often use tape to collect fibers from a crime scene or a suspect's clothes. The fibers are taken to a police lab and examined under a microscope. Fibers that look similar to the human eye look very different under a microscope. Microscopes make it easy to tell wool, cotton, nylon, polyester, and other types of fibers from one another. Bumps and ridges often show up on the strands. If fibers that are found in two different places look the same, they are analyzed chemically to tell whether they may have come from the same place.

Some types of fibers are common, such as those found in blue jeans. These fibers may not be useful to police because they are found nearly everywhere. Other fibers, however, are very rare. They may have been made years ago, or made only in one country. They may be colored by a dye that is not very common. Police try to trace manufacturers to find out who bought products made with their fibers.

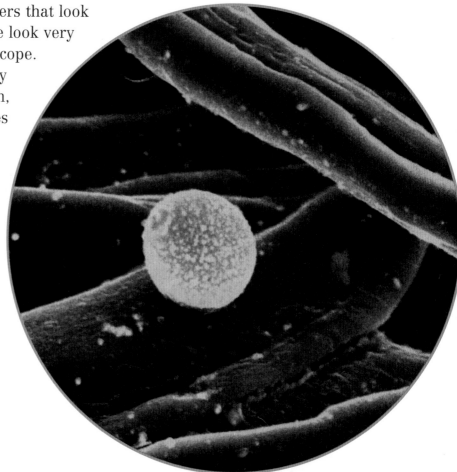

Using a microscope, investigators can see the gunshot residue on this piece of cotton fiber.

How Does Chemistry Help Police Find Clues?

Some types of evidence at a crime scene, such as small amounts of drugs or poison, are impossible to see.

Scientists examine these clues by testing them with chemicals. This process is called **chemical analysis**. Evidence like this can help to solve a case.

Police collect items that might contain valuable chemical clues and take the items back to the police laboratory. Using chemical analysis, scientists figure out if any tiny traces of substances are present.

Some chemical tests show the difference between two similar-looking objects. Although a counterfeit credit card may look like a real card, chemical analysis can show that the two cards are made from different types of plastic.

Police use breathalyzers to tell how much alcohol is in a person's blood.

Blood from a suspect may be chemically analyzed to see if the suspect has been drinking or taking drugs. Blood from a victim may also be analyzed to see if any chemicals contributed to the person's death.

BYTE-SIZED FACT

Police use small machines called breathalyzers to test drivers to see if they have had too much alcohol to drink. The breathalyzer test measures how much alcohol is on the driver's breath. From this figure, police know approximately how much alcohol is in the driver's blood.

How do police use photography to investigate crimes?

At a crime scene, a police photographer takes many photographs to use as evidence. The photographer takes photos of the entire crime scene and close-up photos of any victims. Other types of evidence, including blood stains, footprints, and tire tracks, are also photographed. These photographs later help remind investigators about some of the details they may have forgotten. Photographs may also be used in court to help prove the guilt or innocence of a suspect.

Police photographers also take photos of anyone who has been arrested. These photographs are called mug shots. If a criminal escapes from jail, police sometimes publish mug shots in the newspaper or show them on television. They do this in the hope that someone reading the paper or watching television will recognize the person and come forward to give information that may help police find the criminal.

Taking photographs of each piece of evidence ensures that crucial information, such as the angle of a gun that was dropped, is not forgotten.

BYTE-SIZED FACT
Even evidence that can only be seen under a microscope can be photographed. These pictures are called photomicrographs.

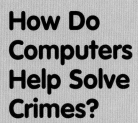

How Do Computers Help Solve Crimes?

Computers are important tools in the fight against crime. Investigators use them to store large amounts of information and to retrieve it quickly and easily.

At one time, all information was recorded on paper and kept in files. Using this storage method meant spending a long time to find one specific file. It is much faster to search for information on a computer. Finding information quickly is important to police investigators. Computers assist police by storing large numbers and different types of records.

Computers allow police officers in one city to research criminals across the country quickly and efficiently.

Many investigating organizations keep computer databases that contain information about people's DNA and fingerprints. This information is easy for investigators to find, and may greatly speed up the investigation. For example, if a fingerprint is found at a crime scene, a computer quickly compares it to the thousands of fingerprints on record. If a match is found, the police may have found their culprit. Before computers, this type of search was done by hand. Police spent hundreds of hours trying to match a fingerprint from a crime scene with the hundreds of fingerprints on record. Computers now do this search in just a few minutes.

Computers help police in other ways as well. Using computers, police can find addresses, owners of vehicles, and even photos of criminals in seconds. Police can quickly receive helpful information from other police agencies around the world. Some computer programs can determine what a missing person might look like after several years. If a young child disappeared 10 years ago, for instance, a computer program would be able to show what that child might look like now. This can be useful in helping to find the child.

Identifying Suspects and Victims

"Tell me everything you can recall."

During a criminal investigation, the most important task is to figure out who committed the crime. This is done by collecting evidence and talking to witnesses. In order to find a suspect, police listen to descriptions given by witnesses. Police use these descriptions to help find details on the suspects. Once police have a suspect, there are many ways in which science helps them to decide whether that person could have committed the crime. Similarly, when people are murdered, it is sometimes difficult to identify them. Police use many of the same techniques to find the name of a victim.

Can police tell whether a suspect is lying?

Most of us have been raised to believe that it is wrong to lie. We usually feel guilty when we do not tell the truth. When we lie, our body language often gives us away. We turn our eyes away and start to fidget. Many things also happen inside our bodies when we lie. For example, we may start to perspire, and our hearts may beat faster.

Scientists invented a lie detector machine that keeps track of these internal body changes. Lie detectors, also called **polygraph** machines, sometimes help police decide whether or not someone is telling the truth. To do this, a polygraph machine measures breathing rate, pulse rate, blood pressure, and sweat production. A person is hooked up to the polygraph and then asked several questions. If the person lies when answering some of the questions, the machine measures changes in the pulse rate and other body functions.

Although polygraphs are useful to police, they are not perfect. Some people are able to lie without any physical changes. Other people are so nervous that they experience many physical changes even when they are telling the truth. The test could show that they are lying when they are not. Some countries allow the results of lie detectors to be used against suspected criminals in court. Other countries do not believe that the results from polygraphs can always be trusted, and do not allow such tests to be used as evidence.

Lie detectors measure the internal body changes that may show whether or not a person is lying.

How do fingerprints help solve crimes?

No two people in the world have the same fingerprints. Even identical twins who look exactly alike have different fingerprints. Fingerprints are one of the most important tools that investigators have to help them solve crimes.

The use of fingerprints to solve crimes began in the 1880s. A British scientist named Sir Francis Galton developed a method to help police use fingerprints to identify criminals.

There are natural oils on our skin that rub off on everything we touch. Every time we touch something with our hands, we leave an image of our fingerprints. Most of the time, fingerprints that are left on objects are invisible. Scientists have learned how to make the prints visible and collect samples that they can analyze.

Fingerprints can be used to prove that a suspected criminal was at the crime scene. If a suspect claims never to have been at the crime scene, a good matching fingerprint is absolute proof that the suspect is lying. If fingerprints are found on a weapon, they may help to identify the person who used the weapon to commit a crime.

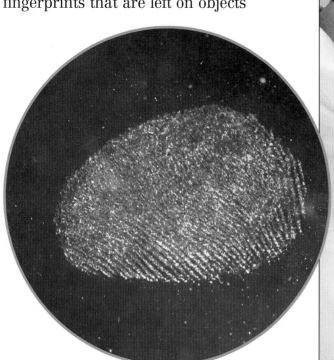

Whenever a person touches something with his or her fingers, a fingerprint unique to that person is left on the object. Police use technology to collect and analyze these fingerprints.

How do police find and collect fingerprints?

One of the first tasks at a crime scene is to find fingerprints. There are two different methods to do this.

The first method is to dust any areas that may have fingerprints. Usually a fine dusting powder containing aluminum is used. Aluminum is a metal that reflects light, so it makes the fingerprints easier to see and to photograph. Aluminum dusting powder also shows up against both light and dark backgrounds.

After dusting, fingerprints are collected in two ways. They are photographed with a zoom lens on a camera, or lifted off the surface. To lift fingerprints, police place a piece of transparent tape on the dusted print. When the tape is carefully peeled off, the image of the fingerprint in the dust is transferred to the tape. The tape of the fingerprint is then placed on a piece of paper or cardboard. It is then either photographed or taken back to the police laboratory.

The second method police use to find fingerprints is to illuminate surfaces with a laser. A laser is a powerful beam of light. When the laser lights up an area, certain substances in fingerprints

Police collect items that may have been touched by the criminal and dust them for fingerprints. The fingerprints are then taken back to the police lab for analysis.

make them glow. Lasers work well to help find fingerprints that are spread out over a large area. Often, a laser will show fingerprints in a place where a police officer may not have thought to look.

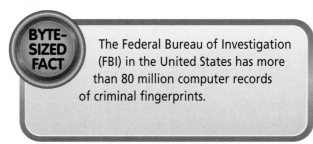

BYTE-SIZED FACT

The Federal Bureau of Investigation (FBI) in the United States has more than 80 million computer records of criminal fingerprints.

What is genetic fingerprinting?

Some criminals wear gloves while they commit a crime so that they will not leave fingerprints behind. Most of the time, however, criminals leave behind some trace of themselves in the form of hair, blood, or saliva. A thief breaking into a building, for example, may leave a drop of blood after breaking a window to enter. Tiny clues like these can help police find a criminal.

DNA, or deoxyribonucleic acid, is found in most cells of every living thing. DNA contains all of the information that makes one living thing different from another. The color of our eyes and hair,

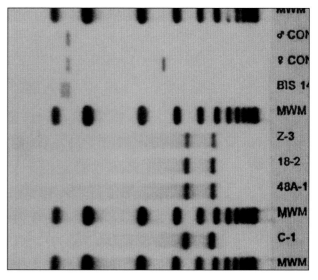

A printout shows the pattern of a suspect's DNA.

An analyst in a police laboratory uses a complex procedure to examine blood samples and test their DNA.

for example, is coded within our own DNA. Except for identical twins, every person in the world has different DNA.

Police take all samples of blood, hair, and other bodily traces from the crime scene. Not all samples contain DNA. Hair, for example, does not contain DNA unless the piece of hair has a root from the scalp on the end. Once cell samples that contain DNA have been found, forensic scientists test them using a special technique. The results of this test give a "picture" or "fingerprint" of a person's DNA. If the genetic fingerprint found in the evidence matches that of a suspect, the chances are good that police have found the right person.

Genetic fingerprinting is not just used to find criminals. It is also used to identify dead bodies, and to prove that someone is innocent of a crime.

POINTS OF VIEW

Should a Government Collect DNA From All of Its Citizens?

Many countries keep records of fingerprints of anyone who is arrested. These records are entered into a large database. Crimes have been solved by using fingerprint databases. Recently, Canada, Great Britain, and the United States have started to collect and keep records of criminals' DNA. With these records, the police can often prove who committed a crime. The United States has even started to collect DNA from noncriminals, such as men and women in the armed forces. The people collecting the DNA say that this measure will help identify any members of the armed forces who die in wartime. Some people want to make a registry of the DNA of all citizens. Other people do not agree with the idea of collecting DNA from everyone. They believe that by providing DNA samples, people cannot protect their privacy.

"DNA sampling is much more intrusive than fingerprinting. Fingerprinting identifies you. DNA reveals quite a bit more about you—your medical history, your genetic code." **Government official**

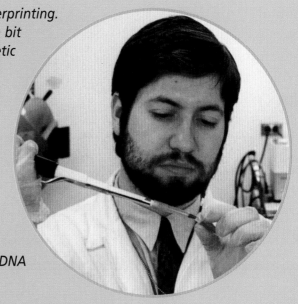

"Why should DNA sampling be different than fingerprinting? Someone convicted of a serious offense should not have the same rights as the rest of us." **Lawyer who represented a man proven innocent by DNA testing**

"Imagine that someone is charged with a break-and-enter [B&E], then released on bail, and the police didn't get his DNA. In the meantime, he knows that he'll be convicted of the B&E and his DNA taken. Do you think he'll stick around?" **Director of a National Police Association**

"Using DNA databanks effectively does not require taking samples from all citizens.... We don't need to test more people; we need more labs testing more crime scenes." **Commissioner on New York's Forensic Science Review Board**

How do you feel about the idea of collecting DNA from every person?
How about collecting DNA from everyone convicted of a crime?
Make sure that you understand both sides of the issue before you decide.

What are blood types?

Genetic fingerprinting is useful in helping prove a suspect's guilt or innocence. However, testing DNA takes a great deal of time and can be very expensive. Before doing genetic fingerprinting, police usually check the type of blood that has been found at a crime scene and the blood of the victims and suspects.

Although blood from different people looks the same, it can be quite different. Scientists can quickly tell if blood is from a human or from an animal. If they find human blood, they look at many different parts of blood cells to determine the blood's group, or type. One way to distinguish between different

types of blood is to use the **ABO system**. In this system, all human blood is divided into four types: A, B, AB, and O. Each person's blood is one of these types.

Millions of people in the world have the same blood types, so the ABO system is not always useful in a criminal investigation. If two people have the same blood type, there are other chemicals in the blood that may help scientists tell from whom the blood sample came.

Blood tests are used to test the source of a sample found at a crime scene.

BYTE-SIZED FACT

In a medical emergency, people may need blood to survive. Mixing blood types can kill the person who receives blood. Type O blood is the only type that can be given to anyone. However, people with type O blood must receive type O blood.

What are voiceprints?

Each of us has a unique way of speaking. Like our fingerprints, our speech habits are different from those of other people. Even if someone disguises his or her voice, the same speech patterns are present.

In certain crimes, police sometimes have a recording of voices as evidence. Obscene telephone calls, bomb threats, and ransom demands are often recorded over the telephone. Scientists listen to different voice recordings to figure out whether they were spoken by the same person.

To compare voices, scientists take two sample recordings and analyze them with a **sound spectrograph**. This machine creates a voiceprint of each of the taped voices. Voiceprints are graphs made of the voice sounds recorded on tape. Scientists then examine the voiceprints for similarities.

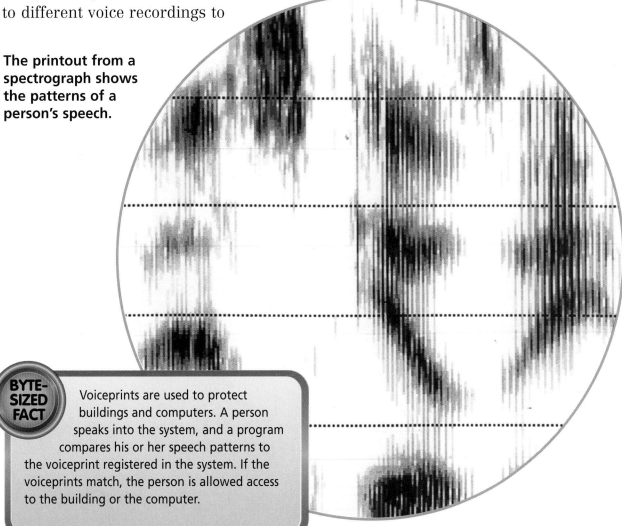

The printout from a spectrograph shows the patterns of a person's speech.

BYTE-SIZED FACT

Voiceprints are used to protect buildings and computers. A person speaks into the system, and a program compares his or her speech patterns to the voiceprint registered in the system. If the voiceprints match, the person is allowed access to the building or the computer.

Can Forensic Science Identify Innocent People?

Forensic science does not just protect society by helping police to catch criminals. Forensic science helps prosecutors prove a case against a suspect. It can also help prove that a suspect is innocent of a crime.

Sometimes police arrest a person they suspect committed a crime. Despite all of their hard work, police sometimes make mistakes. Witnesses identify the wrong person, or evidence points in the wrong direction. When this happens, an innocent person can be arrested and even be sent

Canadian Guy Paul Morin was wrongly convicted of the murder of a young girl. He was later able to prove his innocence using DNA evidence taken from the crime scene.

to jail for a crime that he or she did not commit.

If a mistake happens, forensic science can help prove innocence. This is done by taking different kinds of samples from the suspect and comparing them to those found at the crime scene. For instance, imagine a stabbing victim had blood type B, and both type B and type O were found on the victim's clothing. Police would likely believe that the attacker had blood type O. If they had a suspect with another blood

type, they may conclude that the person is not the attacker.

Genetic fingerprinting has often been used to prove innocence, especially in the case of murders. Scientists have been using DNA fingerprinting techniques since 1984. Some people who were sent to jail years before this time were able to prove their innocence when DNA evidence showed they absolutely could not have committed the murder of which they were convicted.

How do police identify a victim from bones?

Sometimes the police have only bones left from a victim. If the teeth are present, they may be compared with dental records to help identify the person. Otherwise, a forensic anthropologist studies the bones to find out information about the victim.

A forensic anthropologist can tell whether bones belong to a man or a woman. Women's bones are smaller than men's bones. Women also have wider pelvic bones than men. If the person ever broke a bone, the healed break will show even after death. Bones give an idea of how tall a person was. Scientists can also guess an age range from bones. Bones of a very old person look different from the bones of a young person.

If a skull is found, forensic anthropologists use plastic or clay to try to make a face on the skull. This is called **facial reconstruction**. Scientists know how thick skin and muscles are on different parts of the face. By building up these areas on the skull, they create a face that looks much like that of the person when he or she was alive. By adding eyes, teeth, and hair, the forensic anthropologist can create a face that may be recognized and identified.

Police can rebuild a face from the skull of a victim. This process of facial reconstruction may lead to identification of the victim.

How do teeth help to identify victims or criminals?

There are slight differences in everybody's teeth. Dental records, which are kept for anyone who has ever been to a dentist, are useful in identifying people. Teeth are not as useful as fingerprints, because dental records change as a person gets older, but dental records can still help find criminals.

Dental records are also useful in identifying victims. If someone has been dead for a long time, or was burned in a fire, all that may be left of that person is some bones and teeth. By matching the teeth to dental records, scientists can often identify the victim. Even if matching dental records cannot be found, much can be learned from teeth. Scientists can guess whether the victim was a man or a woman, because men usually have larger teeth than women. Teeth also give an idea of how old the victim was. Older teeth are usually smoother and more worn down than teeth of younger people.

If a criminal bites something like a piece of food, or another person,

Forensic scientists who specialize in studying teeth are called forensic odontologists. They compare teeth with dental charts to identify people.

an imprint of his or her teeth is left in the object. If police have a suspect, they compare the dental records to the bite mark left at the crime scene. If the two teeth patterns match, they may help prove that the suspect is guilty.

How Does Dirt Help Solve Crimes?

Plants and dirt can help investigators link a suspect to a crime scene.

Although most dirt looks the same, when examined under a microscope, dirt from different areas contains different things. If dirt found on a suspect's shoes or car tires matches the dirt found at the crime scene, police try to prove that the suspect was at the crime scene. Dirt is also useful for showing footprints or tire tracks.

If footprints are found at a crime scene, investigators photograph the prints and make a plaster cast of them. At the police laboratory, scientists can determine that the prints came from a certain make and size of shoe. They can estimate how much the person weighs by how deep the imprints are in the ground.

Tire tracks in the dirt can help police identify the make and model of a suspect's car.

The design and depth of car tire tracks can sometimes help police figure out the type of car that was used by a suspect.

Plants also help investigators. Pollen, for instance, shows where a person has been.

When people walk through a field, small particles of pollen or dirt may cling to their clothing. By analyzing these particles, police can prove where a person has been.

Pollen is found in most flowering plants. As people walk past plants, pollen sticks to their clothing or shoes. Different places have different types of pollen. If there is pollen on the clothing of a victim or suspect, or if pollen is found at the crime scene, police may be able to use that information to help solve the crime.

How do artists help police investigations?

Witnesses to a crime have seen the suspect, and they probably know what he or she looks like. When this happens, the witness describes the suspect to a police artist. Using the description, the police artist either draws the face on paper, or creates a face with a computer program. The artist emphasizes any of the suspect's unusual features, such as a large nose or buckteeth. The resulting picture is called a **composite**. The witness asks that changes be made to the composite until it looks like the suspect.

Once a composite is completed, police show the picture to other potential witnesses or anyone who might recognize the face. Sometimes composites are printed on posters that describe the crime and ask anyone who recognizes the face to contact police.

Police in California used an artist's sketch (above) to identify and convict a serial killer (left).

BYTE-SIZED FACT

If you are a witness to a crime and the police have a suspect, they may show you several pictures of people who look similar to the suspect. They also include a photograph of the suspect. If you choose their suspect, it helps to confirm that they are after the right person.

What Do Profilers Do?

Sometimes police have evidence of a crime, but they may not have any good leads as to who committed the crime.

If the crime is a serious one, such as murder, the police ask for help from a **psychological profiler**.

Profilers are psychologists who study how criminal minds work. A profiler studies all the details of a crime to come up with an idea of what type of person the killer is. The profiler tries to understand why the criminal committed such a crime. Profilers might decide the sex, age, job, and even habits of the criminal.

The details that the profiler gives to police are compared to descriptions of anyone connected with the crime. If the description fits someone, that person is questioned further.

When police suspect that one person has committed a number of crimes, they sometimes work with a **geographic profiler**. Using information about where the crimes were committed, a geographic profiler can determine where the person who committed the crimes most likely lives.

Geographic profilers try to determine where a suspect might live. Their work starts at the scene of the crime.

BYTE-SIZED FACT

Police investigations can lead to a list of thousands of suspects for one crime. In the case of the "Green River Killer" in the United States, police have collected the names of 18,000 suspects.

Is your home safe from burglars? If someone wants to enter a home, it is possible if enough of an effort is made. However, there are many simple things that make a home safer. To see if your home is safe, try for a moment to think like a burglar. Burglars choose homes that are quick and easy to get into. They try to make sure that they will not get caught. Police recommend that people examine their homes to see if they can be made safer. Safe homes not only protect their inhabitants from crime, but also from fires and other accidents.

What are your answers?

Examine your house outside and inside to see how safe it is.

1. Compare your home to others on your street. If you were a criminal, is there some reason why your home would be more appealing than another? Burglars often look for homes that have hiding spots, such as trees or bushes near doors or windows. This means that they have a better chance of breaking into a home without being seen. If your home looks more expensive than others around it, a burglar might assume that there are more objects of value inside.

2. Examine the locks on your doors and windows. Do your doors have locks only on the handles, or do they also have stronger deadbolt locks? Do all of your windows lock? Are any windows easy to get to by climbing on something nearby? Many burglars enter homes through unlocked doors and windows. Do you keep your doors and windows locked?

3. Do you have a fire or smoke alarm in your house? If you do, check to see that it still works and that the batteries are operating. Does your family have an escape plan in case of a fire? Do you know what you would do in an emergency?

4. Can you find electrical wires that are broken or frayed in your home? These wires are a fire hazard and should be replaced.

Here is your challenge:

You might want to talk to a teacher about having a police officer speak to your class. The officer can talk to the class about ways to stay safer at home, in school, and on the street. Most police officers have very interesting stories to tell, as well.

Fast Facts

1. If all the DNA in a human cell were stretched out, it would be more than 6 feet (2 m) long.

2. Some copier machines are designed to recognize money from many countries. If someone tries to copy money on one of these machines, the copies will come out as blank pieces of paper.

3. In the United States, the FBI has a list of the "top 10 most wanted" criminals in America. The FBI posts photos of the criminals on its website and sends copies to other law enforcement agencies around the world.

4. From knife marks found on a murder victim's bones, scientists can tell what type of knife was used in the crime.

5. Forgeries are often made of expensive perfumes. These perfumes use much less expensive ingredients than the real scent.

6. Some people kill endangered animal species illegally to sell their body parts. An elephant's tusk can bring a poacher thousands of dollars.

7. In a murder investigation, the body is taken away to be studied by a pathologist as soon as possible. Before this is done, police make an outline around the body with chalk or tape. This procedure is done so that police know the exact location of the body in relation to other pieces of evidence.

8. Before fingerprinting was used, police identified people using "man measurement." They believed that it was rare for two people to have the exact same body measurements.

9. Police dogs are trained to attack criminals on command, follow scents, and sniff out drugs or weapons in luggage at airports.

10. Some criminals hide drugs to carry them into another country. Police have found drugs in the hollowed-out heels of shoes and in statues, and taped to legs under clothing.

11. After a fire, investigators use technology to test for gasoline or other chemicals that may have been used to start the fire.

12. Police officers wear uniforms so that the public and other officers recognize them. All police officers also carry identification, and must show it to prove who they are.

13. Police investigating a crime will usually go through garbage at the crime scene and at a suspect's home and workplace, looking for clues.

14. The insects most often found on dead bodies are the larvae of the common bluebottle fly, the greenbottle fly, and the housefly.

15. At the scene of a hit-and-run car accident, police collect any chips of paint left by the car that fled. They analyze the paint to find out what type of car they should look for.

16. Police often collect shoes from suspects to see if the shoes match the size and type of prints left at the crime scene.

17. Since tattoos are permanent, they help police to identify criminals and victims.

18. At one time, it was thought that people could be identified by the shape and size of their ears.

19. Sometimes police dig up, or **exhume**, bodies that have been buried to gather more evidence.

20. Some murders are made to look like suicides. Pathologists can often tell whether or not someone committed suicide by determining the angle of the wound made by a bullet or a knife.

FACT: No two people in the world have the same fingerprints. This makes fingerprinting a valuable tool for law enforcement officers when trying to identify a suspect.

TEST: See how well your crime detection abilities work with this activity.

Looking for Fingerprints

Materials
Ink pad
White paper
Dusting powder (cocoa or chocolate powder)
Paintbrush
Glass
Tape

1. Ask your family members or friends to let you fingerprint them. Press each finger firmly on the ink pad and then on the piece of paper. Label each print with the name of the person and which finger it came from.
2. Find a smooth object, such as a mirror or a glass, that one of your family members has recently touched. With the paintbrush, gently brush some dusting powder onto the object.
3. If you uncover a fingerprint, press a piece of clear tape gently but firmly over the print.
4. Carefully remove the tape, and place it on the white paper.
5. Compare the print to the ones you collected earlier. Can you figure out to which person (and which finger) the print belongs? See if you can find fingerprints on other items around your home.

FACT: It can be proven that a certain person was at the scene of a crime simply from clothing fibers left behind or picked up on his or her clothes. To the human eye, clothing fibers can be either nearly invisible, or they can appear the same as very different fibers. However, we can see huge differences by using a microscope or a magnifying glass.

TEST: Try to identify different fibers in the following activity.

Identifying Clothing Fibers

Materials
Several items made of fabric or woven material
Transparent tape
White paper
Magnifying glass

1. Have someone else remove single fibers from several cloth items with pieces of tape.
2. Tape each fiber to a piece of white paper.
3. Examine each fiber with the magnifying glass. Each fiber will likely be a different color, thickness, and shape.
4. Can you tell from which item each fiber came?

Research on Your Own

To find out more about forensics and crime investigation, check out some of these resources and websites at your local library and on the Internet.

Great Books

Bender, Lionel. *Forensic Detection*. London: Franklin Watts, 1990.

Bowers, Vivien. *Crime Science*. Toronto: Owl Books, 1997.

Graham, Ian. *Crime-Fighting*. Austin, Texas: Raintree Steck-Vaughn, 1995.

Lane, Brian. *Crime & Detection*. London: Dorling Kindersley, 1998.

Otfinoski, Steven. *Whodunit?: Science Solves the Crime*. New York: W.H. Freeman and Company, 1995.

Oxlade, Chris. *Crime Detection*. Crystal Lake, Illinois: Rigby Education, 1997.

Roden, Katie. *Solving International Crime*. Brookfield, Connecticut: Copper Beech Books, 1996.

Sheely, Robert. *Police Lab: Using Science to Solve Crimes*. New York: Silver Moon Press, 1993.

Tesar, Jenny. *Scientific Crime Investigation*. New York: Franklin Watts, 1991.

Great Websites

Activities Exchange—A Case of Murder: A Forensic Science Unit
http://www.gene.com/ae/atg/released/0157-theasinclair/index.html

Forensic Science Web Pages:
http://users.aol.com/murrk/index.htm

FBI Kid's and Youth Educational Page:
http://www.fbi.gov/kids/kids.htm

Glossary

ABO system: A method of dividing all human blood into four different types, depending on what the blood contains

autopsy: An examination of a dead body to determine how the person died, also called a postmortem examination

ballistics: The study of firearms and bullets

chemical analysis: A process in which scientists examine objects to determine what substances they contain

composite: A sketch or image of a person made by a police artist based on a description from a witness

decomposition: A state of decay after death

DNA: The genetic chemical in cells that directs all function and development

evidence: Any clues or details that may help investigators solve a crime

exhume: To dig up a body that has already been buried

facial reconstruction: A method of creating a face by molding clay over the top of a skull

forensic science: Any science that is related to law and can be used as evidence in court

geographic profiler: A person who uses information from crime scenes to determine where a criminal most likely lives

graphology: The study of handwriting

hologram: A three-dimensional image produced by lasers

laser: A strong beam of light

lividity: When a dead body begins to collect blood and darken in areas closer to the ground

metal detector: A machine that senses the presence of metal objects

polygraph: A machine that helps test whether someone is lying or telling the truth

psychological profiler: A scientist, usually a psychologist or a psychiatrist, who tries to determine what type of person committed a crime by examining the evidence

rigor mortis: A temporary stiffness of the body that sets into the muscles after death

sound spectrograph: A machine that makes a voiceprint, or a printout on paper of sounds, from a tape recording

X-ray scanner: A machine that uses X rays to penetrate luggage and other objects to see what is inside

Index